A Reflection of Christ
Journal and Bible Study

Sandie Severnak
Living Life the Lord's Way Ministry

A Reflection of Christ: Journal and Bible Study
Copyright © 2016 Sandra M. Severnak
Living Life the Lord's Way Ministry
www.LivingLifetheLordsWay.org

All rights reserved. Contents may not be reproduced, distributed, copied, or used in any form, electronically or otherwise without permission from the author.

All Scripture quotations, unless otherwise indicated, are taken from the Holy Bible, New International Reader's Version®, NIrV® Copyright © 1995, 1996, 1998, 2014 by Biblica, Inc.™ Used by permission of Zondervan. All rights reserved worldwide. www.zondervan.com The "NIrV" and "New International Reader's Version" are trademarks registered in the United States Patent and Trademark Office by Biblica, Inc.™

Managing Editor: Michael C. Koiner
Cover Design: Michael C. Koiner

ISBN 978-0-9908-0360-7
Printed in the USA

Dedication

This journal is dedicated to all those who seek to draw closer to Jesus. May you remain steadfast in your journey and may your life be pleasing to the Lord.

"Whoever claims to live in him
must walk as Jesus did."

1 John 2:6

Acknowledgement

This journal would not have been put into print had it not been for the encouragement of the women who have journeyed alongside me while we studied the Bible together throughout the years. You truly are women who seek to reflect Christ in all you do. Thank you for abounding in love and grace.

I'm also tremendously grateful to my daughter, Jessica, and son-in-law, Michael, for their willingness to meticulously review the journal and provide Biblical wisdom and insight—and a lot of edits! Their understanding of God's Word and its application transformed this study. Thank you for your love and support. You are both incredible gifts from God.

A Note from the Author

As a Christian, you've been called on a journey to know Jesus, to learn how He wants you to live, and to reflect Him in all you do. But the journey isn't easy. Becoming a reflection of Christ and living life as He did is a great challenge—even to the most righteous of believers.

It's only through the work of the Holy Spirit that we can become more like Him. "As the Spirit of the Lord works within us, we become more and more like Him and reflect His glory even more." (2 Cor 3:18b NLT).

Prayerfully, as you use this journal and study, your understanding of the character of Christ will deepen, your reflection of Him will strengthen, and your walk will exhibit evidence of your living life the LORD's way.

Walking alongside you,

Sandie

Introduction

How are we to live our lives? Whose standards are we to live by? How do we know these standards are the *right* standards?

There are many opinions about how life should be lived and the principles that should guide us. The inconsistencies of values can cause great confusion to those trying to determine right from wrong and live an upright life. Who should we listen to? Who's right?

Navigating life well requires truth, insight, and wisdom. Where or to whom do we turn for guidance and direction? Are we simply guessing at what's good and righteous—or worse—following how the world says we should live? Oftentimes we rely on those around us for advice, support, and guidance. Whether that's good or not depends on what or who those people's standards and values are based upon.

As Christians, we know where to turn. We are blessed to know Jesus is The Way, The Truth, and the Life (John 14:6) and we have a resource to teach us His ways and guide us—the Bible. "All Scripture is God-breathed and is useful for teaching, rebuking, correcting, and training in righteousness." (2 Tim 3:16).

What a gift it is to know that our standard for what is good, just, righteous, and trustworthy come from God Himself, as evidenced by Jesus ("The Word became flesh and made His dwelling among us." John 1:14). We don't have to question the source. Our hearts do not have to be unsettled or troubled when we follow the values provided through God's Word. What a relief! How comforting.

Yet there remains a challenge. To live a life according to the LORD's standards, we need to know God's Word (the Bible), understand His teachings, invite the Holy Spirit to speak to us and guide us daily, and then apply His principles in our lives. Learning about Jesus is a matter of spending time with Him—in worship, in the Bible, in fellowship with others who are on the same path to knowing Him, and in deliberate application of what we've learned.

This requires commitment, diligence, and help. It's no small task, but we can succeed with the Holy Spirit strengthening us and leading the way, and with a few simple tools. This journal and study is intended to do just that—help you learn who Jesus is and provide a path for you to live your life in a way that's a reflection of Him.

The Journal

A Reflection of Christ will help you grow in three ways. First, you'll learn about attributes and principles that God calls us to reflect. You'll also have an opportunity to consider how your life reflects these characteristics and how you can grow to become a greater reflection of Christ. And finally, the journal will actively engage you in developing a daily habit of spending time in God's Word.

It's important to mention that this journal is not intended to encourage a works-based relationship with God. ("For it is by grace you have been saved, through faith—and this is not from yourselves, it is the gift of God—not by works, so that no one can boast." Eph. 8-9). The hope is that as you complete the study you'll be drawn closer to the heart of Jesus through the process called sanctification. "Sanctification is a progressive work of God and man that makes us more and more free from sin and like Christ in our actual lives." (Grudem, *Systematic Theology*, 746). It is the progression of holiness in a believer's life—the outward and inward reflection of Christ—something we are called to diligently work on throughout our lives. So rather than providing a list of behaviors you need to do or not do, or a track record of "I've been good" versus "I've been bad," this journey is about a change of heart—a change from within. The desired outcome is that as you progress through the journal something deep within you begins to change and your thinking and doing naturally and without prompting become more like Jesus'.

What's Inside?

The journal provides a study of twenty-five **attributes** and godly characteristics. For each attribute, there are five sets of Scripture passages, reflection/life application questions, and prayers. If you wish to go deeper, you may read the *Going Deeper* verses that are referenced.

Following the Scripture readings, questions, and prayers, you'll find the ***Reflect and Respond*** and *Life Focus Review* sections. These tools will guide you through a review of the attribute and prompt you to consider areas in your life where you might need to focus more deeply in the application of the attribute. This time of self-reflection is where deep spiritual growth and life-change can occur, so plan to spend a good amount of time here. At the end of each attribute section there's a place for your ***notes*** from your quiet time, Bible reading, Sunday School, sermons, and a section to record ***prayer requests***.

After every fifth attribute, you'll encounter a ***Reflect Back*** section. This section provides a review of the last five attributes studied and will help you assess the progress of your journey.

Study Options

There are two options for completing the study. The option you choose will depend on how much time per day you wish to devote to your study.

5 Week Study—25 to 30 minutes per day
- **Reading:** One attribute topic per **day** which includes five Scriptures, five questions, and five prayers
- **Exercises:** Complete the *Reflect and Respond* and *Life Focus Review* Sections each day.

25 Week Study—2 to 5 minutes per day
- **Reading:** One attribute topic per **week**—read one Scripture, one question, and one prayer per day.
- **Exercises:** Complete the *Reflect and Respond* and *Life Focus Review* Sections at the end of the week.

Group Facilitation

The Reflection of Christ is ideal for accountability groups, small group Bible Studies, and Sunday school classes. The guidelines and schedule are based on a 60-minute meeting.

Select a Reading Plan
Decide whether your group will read one attribute per day (5-week study option) or one attribute per week (25-week study option). Complete the reading prior to the group gathering.

Group Gathering (based on 60-minutes)
- Welcome and Opening Prayer: 5 minutes
- Group Discussion: 50 minutes
    - *Attribute Review:* 5 minutes. Read aloud the description provided for the attribute. If you have more than 60 minutes, ask the group to share which Scripture, questions, or prayers they found most impactful.
    - *Reflect and Respond Review:* 15 minutes. Be sure to focus on this section as this is where life application takes place. Ask members to share how the reading impacted them and what plans they've made to strengthen the attribute. (If using the 5-week plan, allocate 3 minutes per attribute. To manage time and control conversation, you might find it helpful to assign one person to share per attribute).
    - *Life Focus Review.* 30 minutes. Invite members to share their successes, struggles and the spiritual walk goals they've set for the coming week. Listen for ways to encourage, offer guidance, and support. If a group member is struggling in a specific area, and if you have more than 60-minutes, stop and search Scripture together. Or invite the group to search Scripture in the upcoming week and email the verses to one another. If your members are an accountability group, note any requests from those who specifically ask to be held accountable to the spiritual walk goals they've set.

- *Prayer Requests/Closing Prayer*: 5 minutes. Space has been provided on the last page of each attribute section to record payer requests. Encourage members to note the requests and to pray for the needs during the upcoming week. If your group is large or if prayer requests require more time than is available, distribute note cards at the beginning of the meeting so members may write their requests. Collect the cards prior to the end of the meeting. The cards can be read by the facilitator or a scribe can email the requests to the group after the meeting (see section below on *Guidelines for Establishing a Godly Prayer Forum*). Close the meeting with prayer.

Guidelines for Building Meaningful Relationships

Encourage participants to follow-up with other group members during the week. Utilize group text messaging or create a private Facebook group for the term of the study. At the next meeting during the fellowship time, leaders should make it their goal to check in with each member who had a prayer request the prior week. If the group is large, appoint a prayer/care team to be responsible for connecting with each person.

Guidelines for Establishing a Godly Prayer Forum

It's important during your first meeting to establish guidelines regarding prayer requests.

- Prayer requests should never be a forum for gossip or public grumbling. If gossip or grumbling begins to occur, since you've laid out the ground rules in advance, you can kindly and in love say something like, "I can see this is really upsetting you. Here's a prayer request card. Why don't you write down your request as to how we can specifically pray about this situation." Then the request can be handled appropriately without contributing to gossip or grumbling.
- Confidentiality, respect, and privacy should always be maintained. Make it a rule that no details of another person's life may be shared through a prayer request that does not directly involve the person sharing the request or if permission to share the information has not been given. Use the same strategy as above. If you find the

same person is repeatedly exposing confidential information about others, find time before or after your gathering to share your concerns with the person and offer support to help them appropriately verbalize their concerns without their breaking the confidentiality of the other person involved.
- If someone has a genuine concern but permission has not been given to share the matter with others, then the prayer request should be presented as "I have a burden on my heart for someone and request prayers for God's love, mercy and peace in the situation this coming week." No details and no names are to be provided.
- Be sure to get permission from members before emailing prayer requests (allow members to opt-out of the email and/or exclude their prayer request).

A Reflection of Christ

Holy………………………………………………………..	1
Loving……………………………………………………….	7
Forgiving……………………………………………………	13
Obedient……………………………………………………	19
Prayerful…………………………………………………..	25
Full of Faith………………………………………………	33
Merciful…………………………………………………….	39
Righteous…………………………………………………	45
Wise…………………………………………………………	51
Pure………………………………………………………….	57
Peaceable…………………………………………………	65
Humble…………………………………………………….	71
Patient……………………………………………………..	77
Compassionate…………………………………………	83
Comforting……………………………………………….	89
Truthful……………………………………………………	97
Courageous………………………………………………	103
Joyful……………………………………………………….	109
Goodness………………………………………………….	115
Honest……………………………………………………..	121
Gracious…………………………………………………..	129
Honorable………………………………………………..	135
Perseverant……………………………………………..	141
Submissive……………………………………………….	147
Encouraging…………………………………………….	153

Holy

God is Holy, perfect, sinless. God calls us to be *holy*. We cannot be perfect and we will never be without sin. So, what does it mean to be holy people?

To be holy people means to be set apart and different than others because we follow a Holy God. We become holy people when we ask God for forgiveness for our sin, accept Christ as our Savior, by living a pure life, and by serving God and His people.

HOLY: ONE

> *"For he chose us in him before the creation of the world
> to be holy and blameless in his sight."*
> Ephesians 1:4   Going Deeper: Ephesians 1:3-14

The LORD made you holy through your faith in Christ and the indwelling of the Holy Spirit. Record the details of when and what influenced you to become a Christian and a child of God.

Thank God for sending His Son to die so that you could be holy, set apart, and forgiven of your sins.

HOLY: TWO

> *"But just as he who called you is holy, so be holy in all you do."*
> 1 Peter 1:15   Going Deeper: 1 Peter 1:13-16, Leviticus 20:7

How are you different because you are a Christian (a holy child of God)?

Pray that God would strengthen you so that you reflect His holiness in all you do.

HOLY: THREE

"Without holiness no one will see the Lord."
Hebrews 12:14b   Going Deeper: Hebrews 12:14-16a, Ephesians 5:3

How must we be made holy in order to see God? See Psalm 24:3-6.

Thank God for His sanctifying work and for calling you to be holy like Him so that you may one day be with Him.

HOLY: FOUR

"Let us purify ourselves from everything that contaminates body and spirit, perfecting holiness out of reverence for God."
2 Corinthians 7:1   Going Deeper: 2 Corinthians 6:16b-7:1

What are you encountering in your life that might be *contaminating your body and spirit*?

Pray that God would show you how to remove yourself from unholy circumstances or help you maintain your holiness if you cannot remove yourself from the situation.

HOLY: FIVE

*"Offer your bodies as a living sacrifice, holy and pleasing to God—
this is your true and proper worship."*
Romans *12:1*   Going Deeper: Romans 12:1-2

Can you think of a time when you remained holy in an unholy situation? Did you feel closer to God?

Ask God to help you see how pleased He is when you remain holy in spite of social pressures and unholy influence.

HOLY: REFLECT AND RESPOND

What did you learn about the attribute? In what ways were your thoughts, feelings and actions impacted from studying this characteristic?

What specifically can you do to continue to grow in this attribute?

Continue on the next page.

LIFE FOCUS REVIEW

As you seek to become a greater reflection of Christ, consider these areas of your life and respond to the questions below.

- Relationship with God—Worship (Praising God), Prayer Life (Fellowship with God), Scripture Study (Knowing God)
- Marriage/Immediate Family
- Personal Wellness—Sleep, Exercise, Diet, Emotional Health
- Extended Family
- Fellowship and Church Community
- Service to Others—Extended community
- Responsibilities—Work, Homeschooling, Elder care, etc.
- Other

What are some highlights and praises you experienced in these areas recently?

What challenges have you encountered in these areas in the past few days?

In what specific ways could you address these challenges?
Locate Scripture that will encourage and guide you. Discuss with your accountability group so they may support and pray for you.

Notes

Prayer Requests

Loving

God calls us to love unconditionally and sacrificially—without expecting anything in return (agape love). Agape love is pure. Loving God and others in this way is impossible without surrendering our needs, preferences and desires to Jesus and calling upon Him daily to show us how to love unconditionally.

LOVING: ONE

*"Love the Lord your God with all your heart and
with all your soul and with all your mind."*
Matthew 22:37   Going Deeper: Matthew 22:36-40

In what ways do you show your love for Jesus with your heart, soul, and your mind?

Ask Jesus to show you how you can show Him greater love in your heart, soul and mind.

LOVING: TWO

"My command is this: Love each other as I have loved you."
John 15:12   Going Deeper: John 15:9-17

How has Christ shown His love to you? How has Christ called us to love others?

Thank Jesus for the specific ways He has shown His love to you.

LOVING: THREE

> *"By this everyone will know that you are my disciples, if you love one another."*
> John 13:35   Going Deeper: John 13:34-35, 1 John 2:9-11

Can people tell you are a Christian by how you treat others? How specifically?

Pray that the Holy Spirit would provide opportunities to show sacrificial love to others.

LOVING: FOUR

> *"Keep on loving one another as brothers and sisters. Do not forget to show hospitality to strangers, for by so doing some people have shown hospitality to angels without knowing it."*
> Hebrews 13:1-2   Going Deeper: Hebrews 13:1-3

Are you gracious and loving to strangers? How have you shown hospitality to those you don't know?

Ask Jesus to show you how to reach out lovingly to strangers.

LOVING: FIVE

"Above all, love each other deeply, because love covers over a multitude of sins."
1 Peter 4:8   Going Deeper: 1 Peter 4:8-11, Proverbs 10:12

List the people in your life that you need to love more deeply, as Christ loves them. What are some specific ways you can show love to them?

Ask Christ to help you learn to love others as deeply as He loves us, seeing beyond their sinfulness.

LOVING: REFLECT AND RESPOND

What did you learn about the attribute? In what ways were your thoughts, feelings and actions impacted from studying this characteristic?

What specifically can you do to continue to grow in this attribute?

Continue on the next page.

LIFE FOCUS REVIEW

As you seek to become a greater reflection of Christ, consider these areas of your life and respond to the questions below.

- Relationship with God—Worship (Praising God), Prayer Life (Fellowship with God), Scripture Study (Knowing God)
- Marriage/Immediate Family
- Personal Wellness—Sleep, Exercise, Diet, Emotional Health
- Extended Family
- Fellowship and Church Community
- Service to Others—Extended community
- Responsibilities—Work, Homeschooling, Elder care, etc.
- Other

What are some highlights and praises you experienced in these areas recently?

What challenges have you encountered in these areas in the past few days?

In what specific ways could you address these challenges?
Locate Scripture that will encourage and guide you. Discuss with your accountability group so they may support and pray for you.

NOTES

Prayer Requests

Forgiving

Forgiving is the act of letting go of resentment, anger, and the desire to punish when you've been wronged. It's willingly turning the situation over to God and requires humility, love, patience, and sacrifice.

FORGIVING: ONE

"Who is a God like you, who pardons sin and forgives the transgressions of the remnant of his inheritance?"
Micah 7:18   Going Deeper: Micah 7:14-20

In what ways do you feel blessed because you have been forgiven?

Because of Christ's sacrifice, God does not remember your sins from yesterday. Each day you get to begin anew. Thank God and commit to living tomorrow in a way that would please Him.

FORGIVING: TWO

"If we confess our sins, he is faithful and just and will forgive us our sins and purify us from all unrighteousness."
1 John 1:9   Going Deeper: 1 John 1:5-2:6

How do you feel when you've confessed your sin to yourself? To God? To others?

Confess your sins to God. Let Him know you are sorry for the times you've strayed from His ways. Ask Him to give you His power to overcome your sin.

FORGIVING: THREE

"For if you forgive other people when they sin against you, your heavenly Father will also forgive you."
Matthew 6:14   Going Deeper: Matthew 6:11-15

Why is it difficult to forgive others but easy to ask God to forgive us?

Ask God to remind you of the common ground you have with others and to give you a forgiving spirit.

FORGIVING: FOUR

"Be kind and compassionate to one another, forgiving each other, just as in Christ God forgave you."
Ephesians 4:32   Going Deeper: Ephesians 4:31-32

Are you compassionate? Are you forgiving? How have you evidenced this lately?

Ask God to help you be merciful and forgiving to the needs and struggles of others.

FORGIVING: FIVE

"Forgive us our sins, for we also forgive everyone who sins against us."
Luke 11:4   Going Deeper: Luke 3-5, Luke 17:3-4, Matthew 18:21-35

Who specifically do you need to forgive?

Earnestly pray and ask God how to forgive so that no ill-will remains in your heart or mind.

FORGIVING: REFLECT AND RESPOND

What did you learn about the attribute? In what ways were your thoughts, feelings and actions impacted from studying this characteristic?

What specifically can you do to continue to grow in this attribute?

Continue on the next page.

LIFE FOCUS REVIEW

As you seek to become a greater reflection of Christ, consider these areas of your life and respond to the questions below.

- Relationship with God—Worship (Praising God), Prayer Life (Fellowship with God), Scripture Study (Knowing God)
- Marriage/Immediate Family
- Personal Wellness—Sleep, Exercise, Diet, Emotional Health
- Extended Family
- Fellowship and Church Community
- Service to Others—Extended community
- Responsibilities—Work, Homeschooling, Elder care, etc.
- Other

What are some highlights and praises you experienced in these areas recently?

What challenges have you encountered in these areas in the past few days?

In what specific ways could you address these challenges?
Locate Scripture that will encourage and guide you. Discuss with your accountability group so they may support and pray for you.

NOTES

Prayer Requests

Obedient

Biblical obedience is willingly *listening* for God's direction through the prompting of the Holy Spirit and then *following* His will in your thoughts, words, and actions.

OBEDIENT: ONE

"Do not merely listen to the word, and so deceive yourselves. Do what it says."
James 1:22   Going Deeper: James 1:19-27

Obedience to God is shown in part when you listen to, read and study the Word. But you must also apply what is said in your life. In what ways are you being truly obedient to His Word?

Share with God your desires to be fully obedient. Ask Him to reveal specific ways you may be more obedient to Him.

OBEDIENT: TWO

"I am the vine; you are the branches. If you remain in me and I in you, you will bear much fruit; apart from me you can do nothing."
John 15:5   Going Deeper: John 15:1-6

If you abide in Christ, He will nurture and grow you spiritually. What fruit is your life bearing that reveals your relationship with Jesus?

Think of an area of your life where you should be bearing more fruit. Ask God to nurture you so that you might grow in this area.

OBEDIENT: THREE

"You have been set free from sin and have become slaves to righteousness."
Romans 6:18   Going Deeper: Romans 6:16-23

Although you still sin, as a follower of Christ you are no longer a slave to sin. Instead, obedience calls your heart. Think of a recent time when you chose obedience over sin.

Thank Jesus for dying for your sins so that your heart is bound to righteous living and you are no longer a slave to sin.

OBEDIENT: FOUR

"We demolish arguments and every pretension that sets itself up against the knowledge of God, and we take captive every thought to make it obedient to Christ."
2 Corinthians 10:5   Going Deeper: 2 Corinthians 10:3-6

When you have unholy thoughts such as arrogance, pride, or conceit—what can you do to acknowledge and gain control over them?

Ask the Holy Spirit to show you when your thoughts and actions are not pleasing to Him and ask for help keeping your thoughts more obedient to God's ways.

OBEDIENT: Day Five

"...stand the test and be obedient in everything."
2 Corinthians 2:9-11   Going Deeper: 2 Corinthians 2:8-19

Are you obedient in forgiving persons who have caused much pain? Are you able to offer love and comfort to a repentant sinner?

Ask God to strengthen you so that you may remain obedient to Him.

OBEDIENT: Reflect and Respond

What did you learn about the attribute? In what ways were your thoughts, feelings and actions impacted from studying this characteristic?

What specifically can you do to continue to grow in this attribute?

Continue on the next page.

LIFE FOCUS REVIEW

As you seek to become a greater reflection of Christ, consider these areas of your life and respond to the questions below.

- Relationship with God—Worship (Praising God), Prayer Life (Fellowship with God), Scripture Study (Knowing God)
- Marriage/Immediate Family
- Personal Wellness—Sleep, Exercise, Diet, Emotional Health
- Extended Family
- Fellowship and Church Community
- Service to Others—Extended community
- Responsibilities—Work, Homeschooling, Elder care, etc.
- Other

What are some highlights and praises you experienced in these areas recently?

What challenges have you encountered in these areas in the past few days?

In what specific ways could you address these challenges?
Locate Scripture that will encourage and guide you. Discuss with your accountability group so they may support and pray for you.

NOTES

Prayer Requests

Prayerful

Christians are called to be prayerful people. It is through prayer that we are able to fellowship and have a deep personal relationship with God and are able to share our innermost thoughts with Him. Through prayer, we can listen for His will for us, to worship and show our adoration to Him, to ask for forgiveness for our transgressions, to thank Him for His love, sacrifice and care of us, and to offer prayers to Him on behalf of others. Prayer is a gift. It allows us to surrender ourselves to the One who loves us most and wants us to turn to Him for all our needs.

PRAYERFUL: ONE

"If my people, who are called by my name, will humble themselves and pray and seek my face and turn from their wicked ways, then I will hear from heaven, and I will forgive their sin and will heal their land."
2 Chronicles 7:14   Going Deeper: 2 Chronicles 7:12-16

What are some barriers in your life that make it difficult for you to pray as God asks in this passage?

Spend time evaluating what it means to humble yourself, pray, seek God's face, and repent before Him.

PRAYERFUL: TWO

"Do not be anxious about anything, but in every situation, by prayer and petition, with thanksgiving, present your requests to God."
Philippians 4:6   Going Deeper: Philippians 4:4-7

Do you present your requests to God? What is the attitude of your heart?

Petition God to help you overcome what causes you to be anxious. Ask Him to replace anxiety with peace, trust, and understanding.

PRAYERFUL: THREE

"The prayer of a righteous person is powerful and effective."
James 5:16b   Going Deeper: James 5:15-18

Having faith requires you to believe God hears your prayers. How can you remain faithful even though God seems silent?

Pray to have the faith and trust that God will provide for your needs and requests even though it may not turn out as you had expected or desired.

PRAYERFUL: FOUR

"Rejoice always, pray continually, give thanks in all circumstances; for this is God's will for you in Christ Jesus."
1 Thessalonians 5:16-18   Going Deeper: 1 Thessalonians 5:12-18, Luke 18:1-8

You may not be filled with joy at all times, but you can rejoice that God is with you. Do you persevere in prayer even during difficult circumstances?

Pray that God would show you how to rejoice in Him in all circumstances.

PRAYERFUL: FIVE

[Jesus] fell with his face to the ground and prayed, "My Father, if it is possible, may this cup be taken from me. Yet not as I will, but as you will."
Matt 26:39   Going Deeper: Matt 26:36-39

In what areas of your life do you need to say, *Not my will, but your will, God*?

Ask God to align your spirit with His will for your life and pray for the strength to trust Him as His plan unfolds.

PRAYERFUL: REFLECT AND RESPOND

What did you learn about the attribute? In what ways were your thoughts, feelings and actions impacted from studying this characteristic?

What specifically can you do to continue to grow in this attribute?

Continue on the next page.

LIFE FOCUS REVIEW

As you seek to become a greater reflection of Christ, consider these areas of your life and respond to the questions below.

- Relationship with God—Worship (Praising God), Prayer Life (Fellowship with God), Scripture Study (Knowing God)
- Marriage/Immediate Family
- Personal Wellness—Sleep, Exercise, Diet, Emotional Health
- Extended Family
- Fellowship and Church Community
- Service to Others—Extended community
- Responsibilities—Work, Homeschooling, Elder care, etc.
- Other

What are some highlights and praises you experienced in these areas recently?

What challenges have you encountered in these areas in the past few days?

In what specific ways could you address these challenges?
Locate Scripture that will encourage and guide you. Discuss with your accountability group so they may support and pray for you.

Notes

Prayer Requests

Reflect Back

An essential part of long-term, life-impacting personal and spiritual growth is taking time to reflect on what God has been revealing to you about Himself, about you, about others, and about life.

So, it's time to pause to reflect back and review the past five attributes you've studied and assess the progress of your journey. Find a quiet place and take a few moments to flip back through the pages then complete the next page. Consider what you've learned, what you've come to understand, how your life reflects these characteristics now, and how you can continue to grow in these attributes to become an even greater reflection of Christ.

REFLECT BACK REVIEW

The first five attributes you've studied were:

>   Holy
>   Loving
>   Forgiving
>   Obedient
>   Prayerful

How has your level of understanding and appreciation for these characteristics changed as you studied and applied them in your life?

Which do you find easiest to live out? Which are the most challenging?

In what areas of your life have you seen evidence of strength and growth of the attributes? (Refer to the Life Focus sections for insight)

Are there areas that you would specifically like to focus on strengthening in the coming weeks?

Full-of-Faith

To be full of faith means to believe God is who He says He is, to trust in His promises, and have confidence in His goodness in spite of what the world may say or what may happen.

FULL OF FAITH: ONE

"But be sure to fear the Lord and serve him faithfully with all your heart; consider what great things he has done for you."
1 Samuel 12:24   Going Deeper: 1 Samuel 12:24

What great things has God done for you?

Be specific and thank God for all He has done for you.

FULL OF FAITH: TWO

"Now faith is confidence in what we hope for and assurance about what we do not see."
Hebrews 11:1   Going Deeper: Hebrews 11:1-40

What are you struggling with right now that makes it difficult to have strong faith? What steps can you take to build your faith and help you remain confident?

Talk to God about what is currently discouraging you. Ask Him to help restore your faith and provide guidance, encouragement and reassurance.

FULL OF FAITH: THREE

"I do not hide your righteousness in my heart; I speak of your faithfulness and your saving help. I do not conceal your love and your faithfulness from the great assembly."
Psalm 40:10   Going Deeper: Psalm 40:9-11

In what ways is your love for God revealed to others? Do you share how God has moved in your life?

Pray that you will have opportunities to reveal your love for Christ and that by doing so others will be encouraged to follow Him.

FULL OF FAITH: FOUR

"Let those who love the Lord hate evil, for he guards the lives of his faithful ones and delivers them from the hand of the wicked."
Psalm 97:10   Going Deeper: Psalm 97:9-11

Can you recall circumstances in your life where God guarded you from harm?

Thank God for how He has cared for you. Ask God to strengthen your ability to turn from evil.

FULL OF FAITH: Five

"Each of you should use whatever gift you have received to serve others, as faithful stewards of God's grace in its various forms."
1 Peter 4:10   Going Deeper: 1 Peter 4:9-11

What Spiritual gift(s) has God given you? How are you using them to serve others?

Ask God if there are ways He desires you to use your gifts to serve His people that you have not yet considered.

FULL OF FAITH: Reflect and Respond

What did you learn about the attribute? In what ways were your thoughts, feelings and actions impacted from studying this characteristic?

What specifically can you do to continue to grow in this attribute?

Continue on the next page.

LIFE FOCUS REVIEW

As you seek to become a greater reflection of Christ, consider these areas of your life and respond to the questions below.

- Relationship with God—Worship (Praising God), Prayer Life (Fellowship with God), Scripture Study (Knowing God)
- Marriage/Immediate Family
- Personal Wellness—Sleep, Exercise, Diet, Emotional Health
- Extended Family
- Fellowship and Church Community
- Service to Others—Extended community
- Responsibilities—Work, Homeschooling, Elder care, etc.
- Other

What are some highlights and praises you experienced in these areas recently?

What challenges have you encountered in these areas in the past few days?

In what specific ways could you address these challenges?
Locate Scripture that will encourage and guide you. Discuss with your accountability group so they may support and pray for you.

NOTES

Prayer Requests

Merciful

Being merciful means to treat others with compassion, kindness, and forgiveness even when you have reason to be disappointed or angry with their behavior.

MERCIFUL: ONE

"Blessed are the merciful, for they will be shown mercy."
Matthew 5:7   Going Deeper: Matthew 6:3-10

As you show mercy to others, God will show you mercy in return. In what ways has God been merciful to you?

Thank God for His mercy.

MERCIFUL: TWO

"Be merciful, just as your Father is merciful."
Luke 6:36   Going Deeper: Luke 6:27-36

Showing mercy means to be compassionate and forgiving even though you have the power to punish or control. Who have you shown mercy and compassion towards?

Pray that God would help you to be merciful at every opportunity.

MERCIFUL: THREE

"And what does the LORD require of you? To act justly and to love mercy and to walk humbly with your God."

Micah 6:8   Going Deeper: Micah 6:6-8

Who outside your normal social circles can you approach and show mercy to this week?

Ask God to fill your heart with the desire to serve Him even if it means serving outside your comfort zone.

MERCIFUL: FOUR

"The Lord has heard my cry for mercy; the Lord accepts my prayer."

Psalm 6:9   Going Deeper: Psalm 6:1-10

When you falter and sin, do you talk to God about it? What do you say?

Talk to God about the areas in your life where you have sin. Let Him know you are truly sorry and ask Him to remove your guilt and be merciful.

MERCIFUL: FIVE

"Even though I was once a blasphemer and a persecutor and a violent man, I was shown mercy because I acted in ignorance and unbelief."
1 Timothy 1:13   Going Deeper: 1 Timothy 1:12-17

Are there un-believers (those who aren't Christians) in your life who need to be shown mercy? How are mercy and grace related?

Thank God for His mercy and grace in your life.

MERCIFUL: REFLECT AND RESPOND

What did you learn about the attribute? In what ways were your thoughts, feelings and actions impacted from studying this characteristic?

What specifically can you do to continue to grow in this attribute?

Continue on the next page.

LIFE FOCUS REVIEW

As you seek to become a greater reflection of Christ, consider these areas of your life and respond to the questions below.

- Relationship with God—Worship (Praising God), Prayer Life (Fellowship with God), Scripture Study (Knowing God)
- Marriage/Immediate Family
- Personal Wellness—Sleep, Exercise, Diet, Emotional Health
- Extended Family
- Fellowship and Church Community
- Service to Others—Extended community
- Responsibilities—Work, Homeschooling, Elder care, etc.
- Other

What are some highlights and praises you experienced in these areas recently?

What challenges have you encountered in these areas in the past few days?

In what specific ways could you address these challenges?
Locate Scripture that will encourage and guide you. Discuss with your accountability group so they may support and pray for you.

Notes

Prayer Requests

Righteous

A righteous person is one who lives a moral, upright life guided by God's commands.

RIGHTEOUS: ONE

"For the Lord is righteous, he loves justice; the upright will see his face."
Psalm 11:7   Going Deeper: Psalm 11:1-7

There is an earthly and eternal difference between those who do and do not live an upright life. What evidence do you see of the Holy Spirit strengthening and helping you live righteously?

Thank God for providing the Holy Spirit to live in you and to help you live righteously.

RIGHTEOUS: TWO

"Lord, who may dwell in your sacred tent?...The one whose walk is blameless, who does what is righteous...."
Psalm 15:2   Going Deeper: Psalm 15:1-5

One day you will live with God if you've put your faith in Christ. What do you think that will be like?

Thank God for providing a way for you to dwell with Him one day.

RIGHTEOUS: THREE

"...I urge you to live a life worthy of the calling you have received. Be completely humble and gentle; be patient, bearing with one another in love."
Ephesians 4:1-2   Going Deeper: Ephesians 4:1-3

Living righteously unifies people and builds other Christ-like characteristics. In what ways have you been humble, gentle, patient and loving this past week? What affect did your behavior have on others?

Ask God to bless your life with unity as a result of your striving toward righteousness.

RIGHTEOUS: FOUR

"The righteous hate what is false, but the wicked make themselves a stench and bring shame on themselves."
Proverbs 13:5   Going Deeper: 1 John 2:16

Do you find you separate yourself from what is unrighteous or, rather, do you fall into temptation or unrighteousness?

Ask Christ to reveal to you how He walked among the unrighteous but never became unrighteous Himself. Ask Him to show you how to do the same.

RIGHTEOUS: FIVE

"There is no one righteous, not even one.
Romans 3:10   Going Deeper: Romans 3:9-20, Galatians 2:16-21

Since no one is righteous on their own, what does Scripture say about how a believer can be made right with God? What role does keeping the law have in being righteous?

Thank God for His justice that has saved you. Ask Him to help you be a light to the world.

RIGHTEOUS: REFLECT AND RESPOND

What did you learn about the attribute? In what ways were your thoughts, feelings and actions impacted from studying this characteristic?

What specifically can you do to continue to grow in this attribute?

Continue on the next page.

LIFE FOCUS REVIEW

As you seek to become a greater reflection of Christ, consider these areas of your life and respond to the questions below.

- Relationship with God—Worship (Praising God), Prayer Life (Fellowship with God), Scripture Study (Knowing God)
- Marriage/Immediate Family
- Personal Wellness—Sleep, Exercise, Diet, Emotional Health
- Extended Family
- Fellowship and Church Community
- Service to Others—Extended community
- Responsibilities—Work, Homeschooling, Elder care, etc.
- Other

What are some highlights and praises you experienced in these areas recently?

What challenges have you encountered in these areas in the past few days?

In what specific ways could you address these challenges?
Locate Scripture that will encourage and guide you. Discuss with your accountability group so they may support and pray for you.

Notes

Prayer Requests

Wise

A person with knowledge is one who has learned information. A wise person is one who uses their knowledge to discern truth, has sound judgment, exhibits temperance, and does what is right.

WISE: ONE

"The fear of the LORD is the beginning of all wisdom."
Psalm 111:10a   Going Deeper: Job 28:28, Proverbs 1:7, Proverbs 2:1-22

What does it mean to *fear*? In what ways can you replace the *fear* of man (such as the fear of being judged by people, fear of disappointing others, fear of failure, etc.), with the *fear* of the LORD?

Ask God for wisdom and strength to admit the ways you have allowed other things to motivate your behavior rather than Him, His commands, and His values.

WISE: TWO

"Be very careful, then, how you live--not as unwise but as wise."
Ephesians 5:15   Going Deeper: Ephesians 5:15-20, Colossians 4:5-6, Romans 12:2

In what specific ways can you make the most of every opportunity to do the wise thing?

Pray for the Holy Spirit to lead you to discern the wise things in life.

WISE: THREE

> **"Oh, how I love your law! I meditate on it all day long. Your commands are always with me and make me wiser than my enemies."**
> *Psalm 119:97-98   Going Deeper: Psalm 119:97-104*

In what ways have you found keeping God's commands have made you wiser?

Ask Pray that God would continue to reveal the blessings of His laws and commands.

WISE: FOUR

> **"Watch out for false prophets. They come to you in sheep's clothing, but inwardly they are ferocious wolves."**
> *Matthew 7:15   Going Deeper: Matthew 7:15-20*

Do you know God's Word well enough to know if you've encountered false teaching? Give some modern day examples of people in "sheep's clothing".

Pray that God continues to reveal truth to you through the Scripture and protection against false teaching.

WISE: FIVE

"We continually ask God to fill you with the knowledge of his will through all the wisdom and understanding that the Spirit gives...bearing fruit in every good work, growing in the knowledge of God."
Colossians 1:9b-10   Going Deeper: Colossians 1:8-12

What good fruit are you bearing that you know comes from the wisdom, knowledge, and understanding provided by God?

Praise God that He is willing to share His knowledge and wisdom with you so that you may bear good fruit.

WISE: REFLECT AND RESPOND

What did you learn about the attribute? In what ways were your thoughts, feelings and actions impacted from studying this characteristic?

What specifically can you do to continue to grow in this attribute?

Continue on the next page.

LIFE FOCUS REVIEW

As you seek to become a greater reflection of Christ, consider these areas of your life and respond to the questions below.

- Relationship with God—Worship (Praising God), Prayer Life (Fellowship with God), Scripture Study (Knowing God)
- Marriage/Immediate Family
- Personal Wellness—Sleep, Exercise, Diet, Emotional Health
- Extended Family
- Fellowship and Church Community
- Service to Others—Extended community
- Responsibilities—Work, Homeschooling, Elder care, etc.
- Other

What are some highlights and praises you experienced in these areas recently?

What challenges have you encountered in these areas in the past few days?

In what specific ways could you address these challenges?
Locate Scripture that will encourage and guide you. Discuss with your accountability group so they may support and pray for you.

Notes

Prayer Requests

Pure

To be pure is to be free from what is unholy and morally unwholesome. That includes our thoughts, our words and our actions. It's a daunting challenge to control the thoughts we allow our minds to entertain, the words we express in both good and challenging circumstances, and our actions—especially in how we treat others. The choices we make each moment throughout the day determine whether or not we are living a pure life. Through submission, sacrifice, perseverance, and faith we can live more purely today than yesterday.

PURE: ONE

> "Live such good lives among the pagans that, though they accuse you of doing wrong, they may see your good deeds and glorify God on the day he visits us."
>
> 1 Peter 2:12   *Going Deeper: 1 Peter 2:11-12, Galatians 5:16*

Can people tell you're a Christian by the way you live, how you treat others, and you handle your mistakes? How so?

Pray that even when you sin, your actions afterward reveal that you are a follower of Christ.

PURE: TWO

> "Keep your mouth free of perversity; keep corrupt talk far from your lips."
>
> *Proverbs 4:24*

What godly strategies might help you avoid corrupt talk?

There were rare occasions when Jesus became indignant, but he never spoke corruptly. Ask Him to show you how you can speak as He would in challenging situations.

PURE: THREE

> **"Put to death, therefore, whatever belongs to your earthly nature: sexual immorality, impurity, lust, evil desires and greed, which is idolatry."**
> *Colossians 3:5   Going Deeper: Colossians 3:5-10*

Impure thoughts and behaviors drive a wedge between you and God. List the things that are keeping you from a perfect relationship with God.

Pray that the Holy Spirit would help you overcome impurities and to focus more completely on God.

PURE: FOUR

> **"But now you must also rid yourselves of all such things as these: anger, rage, malice, slander, and filthy language from your lips."**
> *Colossians 3:8   Going Deeper: Colossians 3:5-10*

Which of these challenges you most, and why? What can you do to replace this behavior with those that reflect godly ways?

Pray that God would provide you with the strength to replace anger with patience, rage with peace, malice with kindness, and slander with words of encouragement.

PURE: FIVE

"Blessed are the pure in heart, for they will see God."
Matthew 5:8   Going Deeper: Matthew 5:1-12, 2 Timothy 2:22, 1 Peter 1:22

What does it mean to be "pure in heart"? In what areas of your life do you struggle to have a pure heart? What actions can you take to improve these areas?

Pray for a spirit of devotion to Christ, so you will see Him more clearly through the eyes of faith.

PURE: REFLECT AND RESPOND

What did you learn about the attribute? In what ways were your thoughts, feelings and actions impacted from studying this characteristic?

What specifically can you do to continue to grow in this attribute?

Continue on the next page.

LIFE FOCUS REVIEW

As you seek to become a greater reflection of Christ, consider these areas of your life and respond to the questions below.

- Relationship with God—Worship (Praising God), Prayer Life (Fellowship with God), Scripture Study (Knowing God)
- Marriage/Immediate Family
- Personal Wellness—Sleep, Exercise, Diet, Emotional Health
- Extended Family
- Fellowship and Church Community
- Service to Others—Extended community
- Responsibilities—Work, Homeschooling, Elder care, etc.
- Other

What are some highlights and praises you experienced in these areas recently?

What challenges have you encountered in these areas in the past few days?

In what specific ways could you address these challenges?
Locate Scripture that will encourage and guide you. Discuss with your accountability group so they may support and pray for you.

Notes

Prayer Requests

Reflect Back

An essential part of long-term, life-impacting personal and spiritual growth is taking time to reflect on what God has been revealing to you about Himself, about you, about others, and about life.

So, it's time to pause to reflect back and review the past five attributes you've studied and assess the progress of your journey. Find a quiet place and take a few moments to flip back through the pages then complete the next page. Consider what you've learned, what you've come to understand, how your life reflects these characteristics now, and how you can continue to grow in these attributes to become an even greater reflection of Christ.

REFLECT BACK REVIEW

The last five attributes you've studied were:

> Full-of-Faith
> Merciful
> Righteous
> Wise
> Pure

How has your level of understanding and appreciation for these characteristics changed as you studied and applied them in your life?

Which do you find easiest to live out? Which are the most challenging?

In what areas of your life have you seen evidence of strength and growth of the attributes? (Refer to the Life Focus sections for insight)

Are there areas that you would specifically like to focus on strengthening in the coming weeks?

Peaceable

Being peaceable is the conscious act or nature of exchanging anger, frustration, strife, and disagreement with love, understanding, compromise, and grace. To be peaceable means to treat others with respect and to seek unity regardless of our differences.

PEACEABLE: ONE

> "Everyone should be quick to listen, slow to speak and slow to become angry, because human anger does not produce the righteousness that God desires."
> *James 1:19-20   Going Deeper: James 1:19-21, James 3:18*

Describe your listening, speaking, and anger habits? Where do you see improvement is needed?

Ask God to help you replace ungodly habits with those that lead to the righteousness God desires.

PEACEABLE: TWO

> "If it is possible, as far as it depends on you, live at peace with everyone."
> *Romans 12:18   Going Deeper: Romans 12:17-21; Romans 14:19*

What can you do today and in the coming days that would infuse peace into your world?

If it were up to the Enemy, there would be no peace. Thank God for the peace you experience in your life.

PEACEABLE: THREE

> **"Peace I leave with you; my peace I give you. I do not give to you as the world gives. Do not let your hearts be troubled and do not be afraid."**
> *John 14:27   Going Deeper: John 14:25-27, John 18:33, Philippians 4:7*

What is the difference between having heavenly peace and worldly peace? List moments when you have experienced heavenly peace.

Take a moment to abide in the peace of the LORD.

PEACEABLE: FOUR

> **"Let us therefore make every effort to do what leads to peace and to mutual edification."**
> *Romans 14:19   Going Deeper: Romans 13:19; Psalm 34:14*

List some ways you are doing good in the world. How are you impacting others for peace?

Ask God to remove judgment from your heart and provide you with the ability to foster peace with everyone you encounter.

PEACEABLE: FIVE

"Blessed are the peacemakers, for they will be called children of God."
Matthew 5:9   Going Deeper: Matthew 5:8-10

A peacemaker, from a biblical perspective, seeks peace that is based on God's will. When you seek peace, is the process and outcome one that God would support? Is it "your" way or God's way?

Pray that God would allow you the opportunity to practice making peace. Ask for the courage to step into appropriate situations of reconciliation.

PEACEABLE: REFLECT AND RESPOND

What did you learn about the attribute? In what ways were your thoughts, feelings and actions impacted from studying this characteristic?

What specifically can you do to continue to grow in this attribute?

Continue on the next page.

LIFE FOCUS REVIEW

As you seek to become a greater reflection of Christ, consider these areas of your life and respond to the questions below.

- Relationship with God—Worship (Praising God), Prayer Life (Fellowship with God), Scripture Study (Knowing God)
- Marriage/Immediate Family
- Personal Wellness—Sleep, Exercise, Diet, Emotional Health
- Extended Family
- Fellowship and Church Community
- Service to Others—Extended community
- Responsibilities—Work, Homeschooling, Elder care, etc.
- Other

What are some highlights and praises you experienced in these areas recently?

What challenges have you encountered in these areas in the past few days?

In what specific ways could you address these challenges?
Locate Scripture that will encourage and guide you. Discuss with your accountability group so they may support and pray for you.

NOTES

Prayer Requests

Humble

Humble people do not boast or proclaim their abilities or success, but neither are they self-condemning. They modestly acknowledge their blessings by giving credit to God.

HUMBLE: ONE

> "All of you, clothe yourselves with humility toward one another, because, 'God opposes the proud but shows favor to the humble.'"
>
> 1Peter 5:5b   Going Deeper: 1Peter 5:1-7; Proverbs 3:34

Humility does not mean being weak, passive or self-condemning. It means living confidently in who you are in Christ and putting others first. What are some ways you could show humility?

Worship Jesus for being a perfect example of how to live a life of humility while accomplishing great things.

HUMBLE: TWO

> "The Lord does not look at the things people look at. People look at the outward appearance, but the Lord looks at the heart."
>
> 1 Samuel 16:7b   Going Deeper: 1 Samuel 16:1, 6-7; Matthew 23:12; Psalm 44:21

People look at physical beauty, wealth, status, possessions, and power. When God looks at your heart, what "beauty" and "wealth" does He see?

Thank God for the outward blessings you have, for they are gifts from Him. But praise Him for what's in your heart that reflects Christ. Ask Him to make you a greater reflection of Him each day.

HUMBLE: THREE

"Do nothing out of selfish ambition or vain conceit. Rather, in humility value others above yourselves, not looking to your own interests but each of you to the interests of the others."

Philippians 2:3-4   *Going Deeper: Philippians 2:3-8; 1 Corinthians 10:24*

List some of the ways you value others, willingly setting aside your own interests.

It's challenging to always put others first. But as you do, God will provide for your needs in return. Thank God for taking care of your needs as you attend to the needs of others.

HUMBLE: FOUR

"When pride comes, then comes disgrace, but with humility comes wisdom."
Proverbs 11:2

In what recent situations have you seen wisdom through humility?

As you continue to live a Christ-like life, ask God to teach you to have greater humility. In turn you will gain wisdom.

HUMBLE: FIVE

"Who is wise and understanding among you? Let them show it by their good life, by deeds done in the humility that comes from wisdom."
James 3:13   Going Deeper: James 3:13-18

Have you been tempted to practice unspiritual, earthly "humility" that brings attention to yourself? List how you can make them sincere before God and man

Ask God to purify your heart of any selfish ambition or envy that leads to false humility.

HUMBLE: REFLECT AND RESPOND

What did you learn about the attribute? In what ways were your thoughts, feelings and actions impacted from studying this characteristic?

What specifically can you do to continue to grow in this attribute?

Continue on the next page.

LIFE FOCUS REVIEW

As you seek to become a greater reflection of Christ, consider these areas of your life and respond to the questions below.

- Relationship with God—Worship (Praising God), Prayer Life (Fellowship with God), Scripture Study (Knowing God)
- Marriage/Immediate Family
- Personal Wellness—Sleep, Exercise, Diet, Emotional Health
- Extended Family
- Fellowship and Church Community
- Service to Others—Extended community
- Responsibilities—Work, Homeschooling, Elder care, etc.
- Other

What are some highlights and praises you experienced in these areas recently?

What challenges have you encountered in these areas in the past few days?

In what specific ways could you address these challenges?
Locate Scripture that will encourage and guide you. Discuss with your accountability group so they may support and pray for you.

NOTES

Prayer Requests

Patient

Patience is more than being peaceable when something is taking longer than we'd like. Patience means not complaining or giving up during frustrating or difficult times. God commands us to be patient. Why? Because it shows we trust God with our wellbeing, needs, and with the outcome.

PATIENT: ONE

"A person's wisdom yields patience; it is to one's glory to overlook an offense."
Proverbs 19:11 *Going Deeper: Ecclesiastes 7:8*

Do you overlook offenses or do you harbor anger and resentment?

Pray that God would allow you to see a person's heart so you can discern their true intentions. This will help you gain the patience to overlook offenses.

PATIENT: TWO

"Be completely humble and gentle; be patient, bearing with one another in love."
Ephesians 4:2 *Going Deeper: Ephesians 4:1-6*

Think of a recent time when you lost your patience. Which of these attributes (humility, gentleness, love) would have helped you remain patient?

Visualize what it would look like to remain patient and loving during a trying situation. Ask the Holy Spirit to remind you to behave in this manner the next time you become frustrated.

PATIENT: THREE

"Therefore, as God's chosen people, holy and dearly loved, clothe yourselves with compassion, kindness, humility, gentleness and patience."
Colossians 3:12   Going Deeper: Colossians 3:12-14; 2 Corinthians 6:6

You are chosen by God to represent Him in the world. Does that encourage you to be a more patient, compassionate person?

Talk to God about what it means to you to be chosen to represent Him in the world.

PATIENT: FOUR

"But for that very reason I was shown mercy so that in me, the worst of sinners, Christ Jesus might display his immense patience as an example for those who would believe in him and receive eternal life."
1 Timothy 1:16   Going Deeper: 1 Timothy 1:15-17

In what areas of your life do you feel God has been most patient with you?

Ask the Holy Spirit to show you how to overcome the areas in your life where God has had to have the most patience with you, and ask for the same patience with others.

PATIENT: Five

> "Preach the word; be prepared in season and out of season; correct, rebuke and encourage—with great patience and careful instruction."
> 2 Timothy 4:2   Going Deeper: 2 Timothy 4:1-3

When fellow believers struggle to live according to the Scripture, do you offer biblical guidance and encouragement? How patient are you with them?

Ask God to help you be patience, encouraging, and steadfast with fellow believers

PATIENT: Reflect and Respond

What did you learn about the attribute? In what ways were your thoughts, feelings and actions impacted from studying this characteristic?

What specifically can you do to continue to grow in this attribute?

Continue on the next page.

LIFE FOCUS REVIEW

As you seek to become a greater reflection of Christ, consider these areas of your life and respond to the questions below.

- Relationship with God—Worship (Praising God), Prayer Life (Fellowship with God), Scripture Study (Knowing God)
- Marriage/Immediate Family
- Personal Wellness—Sleep, Exercise, Diet, Emotional Health
- Extended Family
- Fellowship and Church Community
- Service to Others—Extended community
- Responsibilities—Work, Homeschooling, Elder care, etc.
- Other

What are some highlights and praises you experienced in these areas recently?

What challenges have you encountered in these areas in the past few days?

In what specific ways could you address these challenges?
Locate Scripture that will encourage and guide you. Discuss with your accountability group so they may support and pray for you.

Notes

Prayer Requests

Compassionate

Compassionate people are those who are concerned for others and emotionally sensitive to their needs. Compassion stirs us to look beyond our personal needs and circumstances and consider the circumstances, condition, and wellbeing of others. Compassion can be either the foundation or the result of love for others.

COMPASSIONATE: ONE

> *"When he saw the crowds, he had compassion on them, because they were harassed and helpless, like sheep without a shepherd."*
> Matthew 9:36   *Going Deeper:* Matthew 9:35-38

What was driving Jesus' compassion in this situation? How can you take part in providing compassion in Jesus' name today?

Thank God for his compassion and forgiveness, for without it, you would be lost and without hope. Ask God to provide an opportunity for you to share His love and compassion with someone this week.

COMPASSIONATE: TWO

> *"Be kind and compassionate to one another, forgiving each other, just as in Christ God forgave you."*
> Ephesians 4:32   *Going Deeper:* Ephesians 4:25-32

How has your level of compassion changed since you became a Christ-follower?

Thank God for the unity of believers, and ask Him to remind others and yourself to be compassionate and tenderhearted.

COMPASSIONATE: THREE

"Carry each other's burdens, and in this way you will fulfill the law of Christ."
Galatians 6:2   Going Deeper: Galatians 6:1-3

What is your reaction when someone reveals they are carrying a burden caused by a sin they've committed? What does the Going Deeper passage above say your reaction should be?

Ask God for compassion and divine wisdom when you are in a position to speak into someone's life about their sin. (Remember to remove the "plank" in your own "eye" first as prompted in Matthew 7:3-5); For guidance, read how Nathan addressed David's sin in 2 Samuel 12).

COMPASSIONATE: FOUR

"Rejoice with those who rejoice; mourn with those who mourn."
Romans 12:15   Going Deeper: Romans 12:14-16

Compassion is having sympathy for someone who is enduring hardship and a desire to help them. How have you recently shown compassion?

Consider those near you who are experiencing hardship. Ask God to show you how you can help.

COMPASSIONATE: FIVE

> *"Do not gloat when your enemy falls; when they stumble,*
> *do not let your heart rejoice...."*
> Proverbs 24:17

God has compassion on us when we stumble. Likewise, we should show the same even for our enemies. How might your compassion help your enemy?

Through God's Word we can find strength to love even our enemies. Thank God for teaching us how to love like Him.

COMPASSIONATE: REFLECT AND RESPOND

What did you learn about the attribute? In what ways were your thoughts, feelings and actions impacted from studying this characteristic?

What specifically can you do to continue to grow in this attribute?

Continue on the next page.

LIFE FOCUS REVIEW

As you seek to become a greater reflection of Christ, consider these areas of your life and respond to the questions below.

- Relationship with God—Worship (Praising God), Prayer Life (Fellowship with God), Scripture Study (Knowing God)
- Marriage/Immediate Family
- Personal Wellness—Sleep, Exercise, Diet, Emotional Health
- Extended Family
- Fellowship and Church Community
- Service to Others—Extended community
- Responsibilities—Work, Homeschooling, Elder care, etc.
- Other

What are some highlights and praises you experienced in these areas recently?

What challenges have you encountered in these areas in the past few days?

In what specific ways could you address these challenges?
Locate Scripture that will encourage and guide you. Discuss with your accountability group so they may support and pray for you.

Notes

Prayer Requests

Comforting

To be comforting is to act upon ones' feelings of compassion (last week's word study) and to help ease discomfort through prayer, companionship, or providing for the physical and emotional wellbeing of another.

COMFORTING: ONE

"Cast your cares on the Lord and he will sustain you; he will never let the righteous be shaken."
Psalm 55:22   Going Deeper: Psalm 55:17-22

What cares and concerns have you been trying to handle that you need to allow the Lord to carry?

Pray that God would increase your trust so that you allow Him to handle your cares, worries and concerns.

COMFORTING: TWO

"Do not be anxious about anything, but in every situation, by prayer and petition, with thanksgiving, present your requests to God."
Philippians 4:6   Going Deeper: Philippians 4:4-9

Jesus experienced many troubles but he was never anxious. He released every problem to His Father. What causes you to be anxious or fearful?

Share these feelings with God. Petition Him to replace your anxiety with peace and trust that He will care for your needs.

COMFORTING: THREE

"The Lord is the stronghold of my life—of whom shall I be afraid?"
Psalm 27:1b   Going Deeper: Psalm 27:1-6

What are some things people rely on for strength rather than God?

Ask God to help you turn to Him as the stronghold in your life and not depend on other means for peace and comfort.

COMFORTING: FOUR

"Therefore, do not worry about tomorrow, for tomorrow will worry about itself."
Matthew 6:34   Going Deeper: Matthew 6:25-34

What future needs are you worried about?

God wants you to plan but not to worry. Ask Him what He wants you to focus on today that may in fact take care of the needs of tomorrow. Then do for today and trust God for the outcome.

COMFORTING: FIVE

"Come to me, all you who are weary and burdened, and I will give you rest."
Matthew 11:28   Going Deeper: Matthew 11:20-30

God wants to carry your burdens. What would you like to give to Him to carry for you?

Let God know you're handing your burdens to Him. Feel Him taking them and giving you peace and rest in return. Now, trust Him to take care of you and go forward in your day.

COMFORTING: REFLECT AND RESPOND

What did you learn about the attribute? In what ways were your thoughts, feelings and actions impacted from studying this characteristic?

What specifically can you do to continue to grow in this attribute?

Continue on the next page.

LIFE FOCUS REVIEW

As you seek to become a greater reflection of Christ, consider these areas of your life and respond to the questions below.

- Relationship with God—Worship (Praising God), Prayer Life (Fellowship with God), Scripture Study (Knowing God)
- Marriage/Immediate Family
- Personal Wellness—Sleep, Exercise, Diet, Emotional Health
- Extended Family
- Fellowship and Church Community
- Service to Others—Extended community
- Responsibilities—Work, Homeschooling, Elder care, etc.
- Other

What are some highlights and praises you experienced in these areas recently?

What challenges have you encountered in these areas in the past few days?

In what specific ways could you address these challenges?
Locate Scripture that will encourage and guide you. Discuss with your accountability group so they may support and pray for you.

Notes

Prayer Requests

Reflect Back

An essential part of long-term, life-impacting personal and spiritual growth is taking time to reflect on what God has been revealing to you about Himself, about you, about others, and about life.

So, it's time to pause to reflect back and review the past five attributes you've studied and assess the progress of your journey. Find a quiet place and take a few moments to flip back through the pages then complete the next page. Consider what you've learned, what you've come to understand, how your life reflects these characteristics now, and how you can continue to grow in these attributes to become an even greater reflection of Christ.

REFLECT BACK REVIEW

The last five attributes you've studied were:

>Peaceable
>Humble
>Patient
>Compassionate
>Comforting

How has your level of understanding and appreciation for these characteristics changed as you studied and applied them in your life?

Which do you find easiest to live out? Which are the most challenging?

In what areas of your life have you seen evidence of strength and growth of the attributes? (Refer to the Life Focus sections for insight)

Are there areas that you would specifically like to focus on strengthening in the coming weeks?

Truthful

The world is filled with deception and lies. Christian's are called to be filled with God's Truth and demonstrate that truth in all we say and do.

TRUTHFUL: ONE

"I am the way, the truth, and the life. No one comes to the Father except through me."
John 14:6   Going Deeper: John 14:1-14

As a Christ-follower, you are also a follower of the Truth. What areas of your life could use some attention as you strive to tell the truth, just as Christ is the Truth?

Thank God for sending Jesus so that we could experience the truth that is hidden from those who have yet to believe.

TRUTHFUL: TWO

"Sanctify them by the truth; your word is truth."
John 17:17   Going Deeper: John 17:1-26

Do you believe the Bible is truth (noun), not just true (adjective)? If so, what truth of the word has most recently impacted you?

Sanctification is a daily process. Pray that the Holy Spirit shows you daily how to live a life that is pleasing to God.

TRUTHFUL: THREE

"Therefore each of you must put off falsehood and speak truthfully to your neighbor, for we are all members of one body."
Ephesians 4:25   Going Deeper: Ephesians 4:17-32

Speaking candidly and truthfully with others can sometimes be difficult. How did Jesus handle this (consider the attributes you've learned in prior weeks)?

Pray that you are able to be truthful and genuine with others and that your words and actions reflect Christ.

TRUTHFUL: FOUR

"Do not withhold your mercy from me, Lord; may your love and truth always protect me."
Psalm 40:11   Going Deeper: Psalm 40:1-17

How does God's truth protect you? List the truths you can think of.

Thank God for His willingness to share His truth (His Word) with us, for without it, we would be lost and without hope.

TRUTHFUL: FIVE

"But whoever lives by the truth comes into the light, so that it may be seen plainly that what he has done has been done through God."
John 3:21   Going Deeper: John 3:16-26

Have you ever spoken or exhibited the truth of God in such a way that others knew that it was Christ showing Himself through you? Explain.

Ask God for wisdom on how to best reveal Christ to others.

TRUTHFUL: REFLECT AND RESPOND

What did you learn about the attribute? In what ways were your thoughts, feelings and actions impacted from studying this characteristic?

What specifically can you do to continue to grow in this attribute?

Continue on the next page.

LIFE FOCUS REVIEW

As you seek to become a greater reflection of Christ, consider these areas of your life and respond to the questions below.

- Relationship with God—Worship (Praising God), Prayer Life (Fellowship with God), Scripture Study (Knowing God)
- Marriage/Immediate Family
- Personal Wellness—Sleep, Exercise, Diet, Emotional Health
- Extended Family
- Fellowship and Church Community
- Service to Others—Extended community
- Responsibilities—Work, Homeschooling, Elder care, etc.
- Other

What are some highlights and praises you experienced in these areas recently?

What challenges have you encountered in these areas in the past few days?

In what specific ways could you address these challenges?
Locate Scripture that will encourage and guide you. Discuss with your accountability group so they may support and pray for you.

NOTES

Prayer Requests

Courageous

Some people are innately more courageous than others. Being courageous or brave, however, is possible for all Christians because we can rely on the promises of God and the Holy Spirit to strengthen us in all circumstances.

COURAGEOUS: ONE

"Be strong and courageous. Do not be afraid; do not be discouraged, for the Lord your God will be with you wherever you go."
Joshua 1:9   Going Deeper: Joshua 1:1-9

What is inhibiting you from being courageous? What is bringing you discouragement?

Talk to God about this verse and where in your life you need courage. Ask Him to help you to be strong and courageous.

COURAGEOUS: TWO

"So do not fear, for I am with you; do not be dismayed, for I am your God. I will strengthen you and help you; I will uphold you with my right hand."
Isaiah 41:10   Going Deeper: Isaiah 41:8-10

God is committed to His chosen people. List some times when you know God held your hand through a troublesome situation.

Pray that the Holy Spirit would help you recall Isaiah 41:10 and the past experiences of His sovereignty when you need encouragement.

COURAGEOUS: THREE

"I can do all things through Christ who strengthens me."
Philippians 4:13   Going Deeper: Philippians 4:10-20

Living life the LORD's way often requires courage beyond our own ability. What are some things that are impossible to overcome without the strength of the Father?

Ask Christ to remind you daily that you are a living sacrifice and that through Him you are able to be courageous.

COURAGEOUS: FOUR

"I eagerly expect and hope that I will in no way be ashamed, but will have sufficient courage so that now as always Christ will be exalted in my body, whether in life or by death."
Philippians 1:20   Going Deeper: Philippians 19-26

What areas of your life need more courage in order to exalt God?

Share with God your desire for Him to replace your weakness with His strength.

COURAGEOUS: FIVE

"They will have no fear of bad news; their hearts are steadfast, trusting in the LORD."
Psalm 112:7   Going Deeper: Psalm 112:1-10

How can faith replace fear during difficult times and increase our courage? Have you witnessed someone who has had great faith during difficult times?

Thank God for being with you always. Take a moment to dwell in His presence.

COURAGEOUS: REFLECT AND RESPOND

What did you learn about the attribute? In what ways were your thoughts, feelings and actions impacted from studying this characteristic?

What specifically can you do to continue to grow in this attribute?

Continue on the next page.

LIFE FOCUS REVIEW

As you seek to become a greater reflection of Christ, consider these areas of your life and respond to the questions below.

- Relationship with God—Worship (Praising God), Prayer Life (Fellowship with God), Scripture Study (Knowing God)
- Marriage/Immediate Family
- Personal Wellness—Sleep, Exercise, Diet, Emotional Health
- Extended Family
- Fellowship and Church Community
- Service to Others—Extended community
- Responsibilities—Work, Homeschooling, Elder care, etc.
- Other

What are some highlights and praises you experienced in these areas recently?

What challenges have you encountered in these areas in the past few days?

In what specific ways could you address these challenges?
Locate Scripture that will encourage and guide you. Discuss with your accountability group so they may support and pray for you.

NOTES

Prayer Requests

Joyful

To be joyful in all circumstances is beyond our own capability. But when we focus on God, His promises, and on our destiny in Christ rather than on our current situation and feelings, we can experience joy that surpasses understanding.

JOYFUL: ONE

"Be joyful in hope, patient in affliction, faithful in prayer."
Romans 12:12   Going Deeper: Romans 12:9-21

The above verse describes some of the marks of Christian love. How would you rank yourself in these three areas?

Practice being faithful in prayer by asking the Lord to fill you with true joy today.

JOYFUL: TWO

"If one part suffers, every part suffers with it; if one part is honored, every part rejoices with it."
1 Corinthians 12:26   Going Deeper: 1 Corinthians 12:12-26

What can you do this week to enhance the joy in someone else's life?

Ask the Holy Spirit to fill you with joy so that you can share it with others.

JOYFUL: THREE

"Consider it pure joy, my brothers and sisters, whenever you face trials of many kinds, because you know that the testing of your faith produces perseverance."
James 1:2-4   Going Deeper: James 1:1-18

Do you trust God enough to choose joy over anger or blame during troubling times?

Ask God for a deeper understanding of inner joy and the ability to express it outwardly during difficult times.

JOYFUL: FOUR

"Until now you have not asked for anything in my name. Ask and you will receive, and your joy will be complete."
John 16:24   Going Deeper: John 16:17-33

Prior to Christ, priests presented the prayers of the people to God. But because Jesus made us right with God, we can now speak to God personally. How can prayer provide complete joy?

Pray and ask God for what is on your heart. Then release the burden of your need to Him and allow Him to replace your burden with joy.

JOYFUL: FIVE

"But the fruit of the Spirit is love, joy, peace, forbearance, kindness, goodness, faithfulness, gentleness and self-control."
Galatians 5:22   Going Deeper: Galatians 5:16-26

We show our Christ-likeness when we evidence the fruit of the Spirit. Which of these do you have well established in your life? Which do you need to work on?

Ask God to help you show joyful evidence of being changed by the Holy Spirit.

JOYFUL: REFLECT AND RESPOND

What did you learn about the attribute? In what ways were your thoughts, feelings and actions impacted from studying this characteristic?

What specifically can you do to continue to grow in this attribute?

Continue on the next page.

LIFE FOCUS REVIEW

As you seek to become a greater reflection of Christ, consider these areas of your life and respond to the questions below.

- Relationship with God—Worship (Praising God), Prayer Life (Fellowship with God), Scripture Study (Knowing God)
- Marriage/Immediate Family
- Personal Wellness—Sleep, Exercise, Diet, Emotional Health
- Extended Family
- Fellowship and Church Community
- Service to Others—Extended community
- Responsibilities—Work, Homeschooling, Elder care, etc.
- Other

What are some highlights and praises you experienced in these areas recently?

What challenges have you encountered in these areas in the past few days?

In what specific ways could you address these challenges?
Locate Scripture that will encourage and guide you. Discuss with your accountability group so they may support and pray for you.

Notes

Prayer Requests

Goodness

Goodness is the quality of placing high value on treating others well and being peaceable, kind, considerate, and virtuous. Genuine goodness is a quality that builds trust and provides a basis for which relationships can be built and strengthened.

GOODNESS: ONE

"He has shown you, O mortal, what is good. And what does the Lord require of you? To act justly and to love mercy and to walk humbly with your God."
Micah 6:8   Going Deeper: Micah 6:3-13

Micah defines goodness in the verse above. In what ways have you recently shown justice, mercy, and humility?

Ask God to change your heart from a pattern of relying on good deeds to satisfy the Lord's requirements to a heart focused on true goodness.

GOODNESS: TWO

"Do not withhold good from those to whom it is due, when it is in your power to act."
Proverbs 3:27   Going Deeper: Proverbs 3:21-35

Do you take the time to do good to others? Who do you need to show goodness to this week?

Pray that the God provides opportunities for you to respond with abundant goodness so that your actions draw attention to God, not to yourself.

GOODNESS: THREE

"A good person leaves an inheritance for their children's children, but a sinner's wealth is stored up for the righteous".
Proverbs 13:22

Our choices, behaviors, and actions impact our life as well as our family's. What inheritance has your goodness built thus far in your life?

Pray that God would help you show goodness at every opportunity.

GOODNESS: FOUR

"Love your enemies, do good to those who hate you, bless those who curse you, pray for those who mistreat you."
Luke 6:27-28   Going Deeper: Luke 6:27-36

Christian love cannot be selective. Consider specific ways you can be Christ-like toward everyone, even those who treat you poorly.

Pray for humility and mercy so you can be good to those who don't deserve it.

GOODNESS: FIVE

"And we know that in all things God works for the good of those who love him, who have been called according to his purpose."
Romans 8:28   Going Deeper: Romans 8:5-30

God's definition of "good" is often not the same as what we expect. List some of the trials you've had and how you experienced God's goodness in the end.

Let the Holy Spirit intercede for your "groans" and inner anxiety during times when you eagerly await eternal freedom from the trials of life.

GOODNESS: REFLECT AND RESPOND

What did you learn about the attribute? In what ways were your thoughts, feelings and actions impacted from studying this characteristic?

What specifically can you do to continue to grow in this attribute?

Continue on the next page.

LIFE FOCUS REVIEW

As you seek to become a greater reflection of Christ, consider these areas of your life and respond to the questions below.

- Relationship with God—Worship (Praising God), Prayer Life (Fellowship with God), Scripture Study (Knowing God)
- Marriage/Immediate Family
- Personal Wellness—Sleep, Exercise, Diet, Emotional Health
- Extended Family
- Fellowship and Church Community
- Service to Others—Extended community
- Responsibilities—Work, Homeschooling, Elder care, etc.
- Other

What are some highlights and praises you experienced in these areas recently?

What challenges have you encountered in these areas in the past few days?

In what specific ways could you address these challenges?
Locate Scripture that will encourage and guide you. Discuss with your accountability group so they may support and pray for you.

NOTES

Prayer Requests

Honest

Honesty is a reflection of ones moral standards. It is based on trust, truth, and fairness and is key to having an authentic relationship. Honesty sometimes requires being vulnerable. Honesty also requires temperance and love when it involves our perceptions and feelings about others. Living a life that reflects honesty requires us to know how Christ modeled honesty.

HONESTY: ONE

"The Lord detests lying lips, but he delights in people who are trustworthy."
Proverbs 12:22   Going Deeper: Proverbs 12:16-19

Words are powerful. How might you handle a situation when being honest is difficult?

Jesus always spoke honestly, but in love. Pray that God would give you courage to always be honest, and the wisdom for how to speak the truth in love.

HONESTY: TWO

"A truthful witness gives honest testimony, but a false witness tells lies."
Proverbs 12:17

Being truthful is challenging at times because we fear more hurt will come of it. But God calls us to be truthful. What damage is done when we are not truthful?

Ask God to strengthen you during situations when being truthful is difficult.

HONESTY: THREE

*"Do not lie to each other, since you have taken off your
old self with its practices."*
Colossians 3:9   Going Deeper: Colossians 3:5-14

Being honest with yourself and God, of which dishonest behaviors do you need to rid yourself?

Confess to God the times you've not been honest. Ask for His forgiveness. Commit to living in truth.

HONESTY: FOUR

*"Kings take pleasure in honest lips; they value the one who
speaks what is right."*
Proverbs 16:13   Going Deeper: Proverbs 16:10-15

Are you honest with the people you lead? In your household, are you modeling honesty for your children? Are you honest with those in authority over you?

Pray that God would help ensure your words are truthful and full of wisdom, especially when you have the opportunity to speak with influential people.

HONESTY: FIVE

"You must have accurate and honest weights and measures, so that you may live long in the land the Lord your God is giving you."
Deuteronomy 25:15   Going Deeper: Deuteronomy 25:13-16

In what ways are you tempted to be dishonest with finances or purchases for your household or business?

Ask the Holy Spirit to convict you of any dishonesty in your life and help you commit to living a life of honesty and integrity.

HONESTY: REFLECT AND RESPOND

What did you learn about the attribute? In what ways were your thoughts, feelings and actions impacted from studying this characteristic?

What specifically can you do to continue to grow in this attribute?

Continue on the next page.

LIFE FOCUS REVIEW

As you seek to become a greater reflection of Christ, consider these areas of your life and respond to the questions below.

- Relationship with God—Worship (Praising God), Prayer Life (Fellowship with God), Scripture Study (Knowing God)
- Marriage/Immediate Family
- Personal Wellness—Sleep, Exercise, Diet, Emotional Health
- Extended Family
- Fellowship and Church Community
- Service to Others—Extended community
- Responsibilities—Work, Homeschooling, Elder care, etc.
- Other

What are some highlights and praises you experienced in these areas recently?

What challenges have you encountered in these areas in the past few days?

In what specific ways could you address these challenges?
Locate Scripture that will encourage and guide you. Discuss with your accountability group so they may support and pray for you.

NOTES

Prayer Requests

Reflect Back

An essential part of long-term, life-impacting personal and spiritual growth is taking time to reflect on what God has been revealing to you about Himself, about you, about others, and about life.

So, it's time to pause to reflect back and review the past five attributes you've studied and assess the progress of your journey. Find a quiet place and take a few moments to flip back through the pages then complete the next page. Consider what you've learned, what you've come to understand, how your life reflects these characteristics now, and how you can continue to grow in these attributes to become an even greater reflection of Christ.

REFLECT BACK REVIEW

The last five attributes you've studied were:

>Truthful
>Courageous
>Joyful
>Goodness
>Honest

How has your level of understanding and appreciation for these characteristics changed as you studied and applied them in your life?

Which do you find easiest to live out? Which are the most challenging?

In what areas of your life have you seen evidence of strength and growth of the attributes? (Refer to the Life Focus sections for insight)

Are there areas that you would specifically like to focus on strengthening in the coming weeks?

Gracious

To fully reflect Jesus, Christians should seek to be gracious—kind, courteous, benevolent, pleasant, polite, and generous. Behaving in a gracious manner comes when one is temperate, wise, patient, and tolerant.

GRACIOUS: ONE

"For it is by grace you have been saved, through faith."
Ephesians 2:8a   Going Deeper: Ephesians 2:1-10

God's grace and your salvation are free gifts through your faith in Christ. How do you show your joy and appreciation for these gifts?

Thank God for His gift of grace. Tell with Him how grateful you are that your salvation is not based on your deeds but on your faith that Jesus died for your sin.

GRACIOUS: TWO

"Let your conversation be always full of grace, seasoned with salt, so that you may know how to answer everyone."
Colossians 4:6   Going Deeper: Colossians 4:1-6

Conversation that is pleasing to God is both gracious and interesting (*seasoned*). How can you add spice (*salt*) to conversation while remaining wholesome and gracious?

Ask God for wisdom so that your conversations are interesting and engaging while also being wholesome and grace-filled.

GRACIOUS: THREE

"Each of you should use whatever gift you have received to serve others, as faithful stewards of God's grace in its various forms."
1 Peter 4:10   Going Deeper: 1 Peter 4:8-11

God wants you to use the gifts (blessings) He has given you to serve others. How are you sharing the gracious gifts God has given you?

Spend time talking to God about how He might wish to use you as a co-worker in the faith.

GRACIOUS: FOUR

"Accept one another, then, just as Christ accepted you, in order to bring praise to God."
Romans 15:7   Going Deeper: Romans 15:1-12

Jesus accepts you even with your flaws. Who do you need to love or show respect to in spite of their flaws?

Consider how Jesus loved and showed respect to outcasts and the unloved. Ask the Holy Spirit to show you how you, too, can love others like Jesus.

GRACIOUS: FIVE

> *"Out of his fullness we have all received grace in place of grace already given."*
> John 1:16   Going Deeper: John 1:14-18

Consider the magnitude of God's grace. How can you share with others the way that God has met your every need?

Thank God for His grace that replaces the law of Moses. Ask God to open your heart to love those who don't know the grace of God.

GRACIOUS: REFLECT AND RESPOND

What did you learn about the attribute? In what ways were your thoughts, feelings and actions impacted from studying this characteristic?

What specifically can you do to continue to grow in this attribute?

Continue on the next page.

LIFE FOCUS REVIEW

As you seek to become a greater reflection of Christ, consider these areas of your life and respond to the questions below.

- Relationship with God—Worship (Praising God), Prayer Life (Fellowship with God), Scripture Study (Knowing God)
- Marriage/Immediate Family
- Personal Wellness—Sleep, Exercise, Diet, Emotional Health
- Extended Family
- Fellowship and Church Community
- Service to Others—Extended community
- Responsibilities—Work, Homeschooling, Elder care, etc.
- Other

What are some highlights and praises you experienced in these areas recently?

What challenges have you encountered in these areas in the past few days?

In what specific ways could you address these challenges?
Locate Scripture that will encourage and guide you. Discuss with your accountability group so they may support and pray for you.

NOTES

Prayer Requests

Honorable

As we mature in our ability to emulate Jesus, we will become more honorable people, who are respected, have a high degree of credibility, and are regarded for our integrity.

HONORABLE: ONE

"Whoever serves me must follow me; and where I am, my servant also will be. My Father will honor the one who serves me."
John 12:26   Going Deeper: John 12:26-35

God will honor you (consider with care, intercede for) when you follow Jesus through respecting His commands, loving others, and sharing the Gospel. Do you believe your life is a reflection of Jesus that's worthy of God's honor (respect)?

Ask God to show you how you can show greater honor to Jesus in your life.

HONORABLE: TWO

"Honor your father and your mother, as the Lord your God has commanded you,"
Deuteronomy 5:16a   Going Deeper: Deuteronomy 5:1-22

How do you show respect to your parents, even when your relationship with them may not be ideal?

Ask the Holy Spirit to show you how to honor your parents the way God wants you to.

HONORABLE: THREE

"Be devoted to one another in love. Honor one another above yourselves."
Romans 12:10   Going Deeper: Romans 12:9-21

What does it mean to *honor one another above yourself*? How specifically should you do this?

As you pray today, ask God to show you what it means to love others as Jesus has loved you.

HONORABLE: FOUR

"You were bought at a price. Therefore honor God with your bodies."
1 Corinthians 6:20   Going Deeper: 1 Corinthians 6:12-20

Do you honor your body by taking care of it? Presenting it respectfully? Outline all the ways the *Going Deeper* passage teaches us about honoring our bodies.

Pray that God would help you honor your body through the outline you made above (such as: rest, appropriate dress, and bodily behavior).

HONORABLE: FIVE

"Honor the Lord with your wealth, with the first-fruits of all your crops;"
Proverbs 3:9   Going Deeper: Proverbs 3:5-12

God asks that you *tithe* as a commitment to Him and to help further His Kingdom. If you are not tithing, what can you do to begin a path to doing so?

All that you have is a gift from God. Giving back to God is an act of worship. Pray that God helps you direct your finances so you are able to give joyfully.

HONORABLE: REFLECT AND RESPOND

What did you learn about the attribute? In what ways were your thoughts, feelings and actions impacted from studying this characteristic?

What specifically can you do to continue to grow in this attribute?

Continue on the next page.

LIFE FOCUS REVIEW

As you seek to become a greater reflection of Christ, consider these areas of your life and respond to the questions below.

- Relationship with God—Worship (Praising God), Prayer Life (Fellowship with God), Scripture Study (Knowing God)
- Marriage/Immediate Family
- Personal Wellness—Sleep, Exercise, Diet, Emotional Health
- Extended Family
- Fellowship and Church Community
- Service to Others—Extended community
- Responsibilities—Work, Homeschooling, Elder care, etc.
- Other

What are some highlights and praises you experienced in these areas recently?

What challenges have you encountered in these areas in the past few days?

In what specific ways could you address these challenges?
Locate Scripture that will encourage and guide you. Discuss with your accountability group so they may support and pray for you.

Notes

Prayer Requests

Perseverant

Everyone experiences difficulties and challenges but, as Christians, we can lean on God to persevere through our circumstances in spite of difficult times. We know God is for us, He is with us, and has provided the Holy Spirit to support and guide us through our challenges.

PERSEVERANT: ONE

"Blessed is the one who perseveres under trial because, having stood the test, that person will receive the crown of life that the Lord has promised to those who love him."
James 1:12   Going Deeper: James 1:2-18

How can you keep the promises and the peace of God above the challenges of this world and persevere in your walk with Christ?

In your times of trial, ask that Christ would come alongside you and show you how to stand strong as He did.

PERSEVERANT: TWO

"We are hard pressed on every side, but not crushed; perplexed, but not in despair; persecuted, but not abandoned; struck down, but not destroyed."
2 Corinthians 4:8-9   Going Deeper: 2 Corinthians 4:1-18

Consider a difficult situation you have or recently had. Which of the strategies mentioned above and in the *Going Deeper* section are you able to apply to the situation that will allow you to persevere?

Pray that God will strengthen you so you aren't overwhelmed and can overcome your challenges in His name.

PERSEVERANT: THREE

> *"...we know that suffering produces perseverance; perseverance, character; and character, hope."*
> Romans 5:3-4   Going Deeper: Romans 5:1-11

How have your sufferings produced perseverance and built your character?

No one wants to suffer. But if we must, ask God to sustain you so that you persevere and produce character that is more like Christ.

PERSEVERANT: FOUR

> *"Therefore, since we are surrounded by such a great cloud of witnesses, let us throw off everything that hinders and the sin that so easily entangles. And let us run with perseverance the race marked out for us,"*
> Hebrews 12:1   Going Deeper: Hebrews 12:1-3

Name some people who have persevered through challenges and maintained their witness as Christians.

Thank God for those in the Bible, in Church history, and in your life who have *run the race* and are a source of encouragement and hope.

PERSEVERANT: FIVE

"By faith he left Egypt, not fearing the king's anger; he persevered because he saw him who is invisible."

Hebrew 11:27   Going Deeper: Exodus 2-4:17

Read the story of Moses in the *Going Deeper* verses. Can you recall a time when you endured hardship but had confidence that God was leading you through it?

Praise God for His sovereignty and for sustaining you during challenging situations.

PERSEVERANT: SIX—REFLECT AND RESPOND

What did you learn about the attribute? In what ways were your thoughts, feelings and actions impacted from studying this characteristic?

What specifically can you do to continue to grow in this attribute?

Continue on the next page.

LIFE FOCUS REVIEW

As you seek to become a greater reflection of Christ, consider these areas of your life and respond to the questions below.

- Relationship with God—Worship (Praising God), Prayer Life (Fellowship with God), Scripture Study (Knowing God)
- Marriage/Immediate Family
- Personal Wellness—Sleep, Exercise, Diet, Emotional Health
- Extended Family
- Fellowship and Church Community
- Service to Others—Extended community
- Responsibilities—Work, Homeschooling, Elder care, etc.
- Other

What are some highlights and praises you experienced in these areas recently?

What challenges have you encountered in these areas in the past few days?

In what specific ways could you address these challenges?
Locate Scripture that will encourage and guide you. Discuss with your accountability group so they may support and pray for you.

NOTES

Prayer Requests

Submissive

The biblical meaning of submission is often misunderstood. This is due, in part, to the world's definition which is far from God's meaning of submission. Understanding submission as God designed is key to our lives as Christians.

When we become a Christian, we choose God through Christ as our leader and authority. It is an act of submission. We commit to allow Him to care for us and guide us. This provides great peace, confidence, and joy because we know God is good, loving, protective, righteous, and pure. And His leadership is motivated by love and draws us nearer to who we were created to be. This is the model that all who are in authority are called to emulate.

When leaders live in accordance with God's ways, we can submit to their authority with peace and confidence as an act of reverence to Jesus. Through submission to godly leaders, we can be peace-filled, loving citizens, spouses, children, parents, employees, and contributors.

Unlike worldly submission, biblical submission is not about forced control, living in fear, belittlement, inferiority, or worthlessness. It is not self-loathing nor does it ignore self-care or self-value.

Biblical submission does not mean you go along with or agree with everything that a person in authority says if it violates Scripture or your conscience as directed by the Holy Spirit. We need to recognize that when submission to one in authority conflicts with God's authority, we are to submit to God's authority above all others.

Sources: Grudem, Wayne. *Systematic Theology*. Grand Rapids: Zondervan, 1994. Print
Miller Kevin A. *"What's So Scary About Submission, Today's Christian Woman.com, Sept 2008,* web
Deffinbaugh, Robert L. (Bob). *"The Glory of Suffering – Studies in 1 Peter",* Bible.org, 2004, web

SUBMISSIVE: ONE

> *"Father, if you are willing, take this cup from me;*
> *yet not my will, but yours be done."*
> Luke 22:42   Going Deeper: Luke 22:39-46

Jesus submitted to God's will under the most extreme circumstances. What experiences have you had where you found it challenging to submit your will to God?

Read the *Going Deeper* verses. God provided Jesus with strength to endure great hardship. When you are in difficult times, submit your will to God and pray fervently. He will give you strength when you need it most.

SUBMISSIVE: TWO

> *"'Our Father in heaven, hallowed be your name, your kingdom come,*
> *your will be done, on earth as it is in heaven.'"*
> Matthew 6:9-10   Going Deeper: Matthew 6:9-13

When we say The Lord's Prayer we are professing our willingness to submit to the will of God. When you say these words, are you actively considering what you need to turn over to God?

Read The Lord's Prayer (Matthew 6:9-13). Ask God to provide you with greater insight as to how you can participate more fully in your submission to His will.

SUBMISSIVE: THREE

"Submit to one another out of reverence for Christ."
Ephesians 5:21   Going Deeper: Ephesians 5:21-33; Philippians 2:1-4

When we submit to God, it reveals our commitment to be like Jesus. Likewise, when we submit to those as specifically instructed by God (read the Going Deeper verses) and give priority to their discernment, concerns, and needs we also model Jesus by putting others first. Do you struggle with this? Why?

Earnestly pray and ask Jesus to show you how you can submit your will more fully and put others needs first.

SUBMISSIVE: FOUR

"Submit yourselves for the Lord's sake to every human authority: whether to the emperor, as the supreme authority, or to governors, who are sent by him to punish those who do wrong and to commend those who do right. For it is God's will that by doing good you should silence the ignorant talk of foolish people."
1 Peter 2:13-15   Going Deeper: 1 Peter 2:11-25

We are commanded to live according to the law of our land, as long as doing so does not go against God's teachings, so that our faith is highly regarded and a witness to unbelievers. Is this a challenge for you to trust God and submit to His plan when those in authority are not living a godly life or are ruling unjustly? How did Jesus handle this situation?

Pray that God would help you trust Him to take care of the injustice and wrongful behavior in the world and to increase your witness, patience, and peace.

SUBMISSIVE: FIVE

"But the wisdom that comes from heaven is first of all pure; then peace-loving, considerate, submissive, full of mercy and good fruit, impartial and sincere."
James 3:17   Going Deeper: James 3:13-18

Our words and actions reveal how fully we've submitted ourselves to Christ-like ways. Are your motives pure? Do you escalate arguments? Do you consider the needs of others before your own? Does your life reveal evidence of your faith? Your responses to these questions will help you evaluate how well you're submitting to God's commands.

It's not easy submitting our will to God. But the result of doing so are far better than living by our own desires. Pray for clarity on how you can turn yourself over to God more fully so you can be an even greater blessing in the world.

SUBMISSIVE: REFLECT AND RESPOND

What did you learn about the attribute? In what ways were your thoughts, feelings and actions impacted from studying this characteristic?

What specifically can you do to continue to grow in this attribute?

Continue on the next page.

LIFE FOCUS REVIEW

As you seek to become a greater reflection of Christ, consider these areas of your life and respond to the questions below.

- Relationship with God—Worship (Praising God), Prayer Life (Fellowship with God), Scripture Study (Knowing God)
- Marriage/Immediate Family
- Personal Wellness—Sleep, Exercise, Diet, Emotional Health
- Extended Family
- Fellowship and Church Community
- Service to Others—Extended community
- Responsibilities—Work, Homeschooling, Elder care, etc.
- Other

What are some highlights and praises you experienced in these areas recently?

What challenges have you encountered in these areas in the past few days?

In what specific ways could you address these challenges?
Locate Scripture that will encourage and guide you. Discuss with your accountability group so they may support and pray for you.

Notes

Prayer Requests

Encouraging

As we live a life that embodies the attributes that reflect God's nature, we will become an encouragement to others through our actions and words. We will be a witness of the power and love of Christ and, with the help of the Holy Spirit, draw others to Him.

ENCOURAGING: ONE

"May the God who gives endurance and encouragement give you the same attitude of mind toward each other that Christ Jesus had."
Romans 15:5   Going Deeper: Romans 15:1-6

Are you an encourager by nature? How can you go beyond your nature to reflect the encouragement of Christ to others?

Ask the Holy Spirit to help you have the attitude of Christ so that you may be an encourager of others.

ENCOURAGING: TWO

"He must hold firmly to the trustworthy message as it has been taught, so that he can encourage others by sound doctrine and refute those who oppose it."
Titus 1:9   Going Deeper: Titus 1:6-9

Encouraging others in sound doctrine is God's command. What are some ways you might share what you are learning about being a Christian?

Ask God to provide you with opportunities to share how Jesus has transformed your life so that they too may grow in discipleship.

ENCOURAGING: THREE

"But encourage one another daily, as long as it is called 'Today,' so that none of you may be hardened by sin's deceitfulness."
Hebrews 3:13   Going Deeper: Hebrews 3:12-14

Encouragement can come in the form of a kind word but also as a warning or reminder. Where do you need such encouragement, and who can you ask for it?

Thank God for the times he allows you to be encouraged through kind words as well as through gentle discipline.

ENCOURAGING: FOUR

"And we urge you, brothers and sisters, warn those who are idle and disruptive, encourage the disheartened, help the weak, be patient with everyone."
1 Thessalonians 5:14   Going Deeper: 1 Thessalonians 5:12-24

List several people who you know could use some encouragement. Make a commitment to reach out to them this week.

Pray that God would help you be sensitive to the needs of others and to be an encourager to them.

ENCOURAGING: FIVE

> *"...encourage one another, be of one mind, live in peace. And the God of love and peace will be with you."*
> 2 Corinthians 13:11b   Going Deeper: 2 Corinthians 13:1-14

If you encouraged everyone you encountered today, do you believe it would contribute to peace and love? Try it and record what you experience.

Ask God to allow you to be a vessel of encouragement, peace and love to your brothers and sisters in Christ so that you might live in unity.

ENCOURAGING: REFLECT AND RESPOND

What did you learn about the attribute? In what ways were your thoughts, feelings and actions impacted from studying this characteristic?

What specifically can you do to continue to grow in this attribute?

ntinue on the next page.

LIFE FOCUS REVIEW

As you seek to become a greater reflection of Christ, consider these areas of your life and respond to the questions below.

- Relationship with God—Worship (Praising God), Prayer Life (Fellowship with God), Scripture Study (Knowing God)
- Marriage/Immediate Family
- Personal Wellness—Sleep, Exercise, Diet, Emotional Health
- Extended Family
- Fellowship and Church Community
- Service to Others—Extended community
- Responsibilities—Work, Homeschooling, Elder care, etc.
- Other

What are some highlights and praises you experienced in these areas recently?

What challenges have you encountered in these areas in the past few days?

In what specific ways could you address these challenges?
Locate Scripture that will encourage and guide you. Discuss with your accountability group so they may support and pray for you.

NOTES

Prayer Requests

Reflect Back

An essential part of long-term, life-impacting personal and spiritual growth is taking time to reflect on what God has been revealing to you about Himself, about you, about others, and about life.

So, it's time to pause to reflect back and review the past five attributes you've studied and assess the progress of your journey. Find a quiet place and take a few moments to flip back through the pages then complete the next page. Consider what you've learned, what you've come to understand, how your life reflects these characteristics now, and how you can continue to grow in these attributes to become an even greater reflection of Christ.

REFLECT BACK REVIEW

The last five attributes you've studied were:

> Gracious
> Honorable
> Perseverant
> Submissive
> Encouraging

How has your level of understanding and appreciation for these characteristics changed as you studied and applied them in your life?

Which do you find easiest to live out? Which are the most challenging?

In what areas of your life have you seen evidence of strength and growth of the attributes? (Refer to the Life Focus sections for insight)

Are there areas that you would specifically like to focus on strengthening in the coming weeks?

Your Journey

There's a reason *encouraging* is the last attribute of this study.

You've spent a great deal of time steeped in learning many of the attributes that are important to God and evidenced by Christ. The hope is that not only have you strengthened your relationship with God, are more aware of how God calls you to live, have a deeper understanding of the Scripture, but also that you are a greater reflection of Christ.

As your life reflects greater Christ-likeness, know that God is pleased. Jesus said, "Now that you know these things, you will be blessed if you do them." What a wonderful promise and encouragement to continue your journey. That's encouraging to you *and* to others. Because, as you exhibit the power of God's transforming love, you'll become an example and others will be encouraged to devote themselves to strengthen their walk as you have.

So, don't stop here. Continue to worship, pray, study Scripture, serve, and spend time with others while applying what you've learned and practiced during your time in this study. Continue to do a "Life Focus Review" regularly—taking stock of your thoughts and actions and testing them against Scripture and the godly attributes you've studied. And finally, share what you've learned with others so you can be an encouragement in their walk. We're all on a journey and need to help one another along the path to living life the Lord's way.

About Living Life the Lord's Way Ministry

Living Life the Lord's Way Ministry's purpose is to help you come to know and understand God's Word in simple and manageable ways, reveal the personal and loving relationship God wants to share with you, provide tools and resources that will help you live your life according to His will, and inspire and uplift you through the joy that comes from following the Lord.

Sandie Severnak, Founder
Living Life the Lord's Way Ministry
www.LivingLifetheLordsWay.org

Made in the USA
Coppell, TX
09 May 2024

32189186R00098